Cryptocurrency Guidebook

Understanding Bitcoin

What You Should Know Before Investing

ISBN-13: 978-1977856623
ISBN-10: 1977856624

TABLE OF CONTENTS

Introduction

About the eBook

This book tries to cut into what cryptocurrency is, with a heavy bias towards where it started: the bitcoin blockchain. We will deliberately avoid technical terminology so we can explain, in as brief and straightforward a manner, what is necessary for the reader to grasp the various concepts, terms, and information required to decide whether to jump into the cryptocurrency world or not.

Many myths exist about what bitcoin and the rest of the currencies are. Most people who talk about cryptocurrencies do not have any idea about how it works. They just know it can be used to do many things, including defrauding other clueless and gullible people of their money, with the promise of quick and hefty returns.

Without any bias, we will try to delve into the advantages and pitfalls that you could land into when you decide to take a leap of faith and invest in cryptocurrencies.

There is money to be made at this nascent stage of blockchain technology. But the risk of losing everything is clear and present.

Read this book to help you mitigate most of the concerns you might have in succeeding in owning and trading in cryptocurrencies.

What you will gain by reading this eBook

After you read this book, you should be able to:

- Identify blockchain terminology and technology
- Get an overview of how cryptocurrencies work
- Get a feel of what is happening concerning cryptocurrency regulation
- Know the various players in cryptocurrency, and how they work together in blockchain communities
- Know the pros and cons of investing in cryptocurrencies
- Get started with online resources where you can get information about cryptocurrencies.

Blockchain: How does it work?

What is a blockchain?

A blockchain is an open digital, decentralized ledger containing economic transactions. Since the internet is a network of interconnected computers, specialized computers can join a community of those that accept to hold a copy of the ledger of transactions that are in a blockchain, and confirm its transactions.

Once there, each computer keeps a copy of the ledger, which then has the responsibility of verifying transactions as they happen, and updating the ledger as appropriate. The computer also receives changes made by other computers and updates its copy of the ledger. To keep nodes powered and online to support a blockchain, the miners are given incentives in the form of mined cryptocurrency or earned transaction fees.

How does it work

Since the internet is a network of computers, a blockchain is adopted by interconnected computers that form a community. These machines are called nodes. They are all then equipped with the latest copy of the database that records all the transactions that happen in the blockchain.

To decentralize the minting of bitcoins and space their production evenly, the developer encodes in the blockchain the responsibility for online computers to find block identities and request whether they are valid. This is called mining. A valid block identity, also known as a hash, is found within a range that is defined to run for roughly two weeks, and the blockchain ensures that only 2016 block identities can be identified in that time.

When a computer finds a hash, it "declares" through what is known as proof of work, and it is rewarded based on the current rate. In 2016, the rate was set at 12.5 bitcoins per hash. This reward is halved every four years, or after approximately 210,000 blocks have been mined. This proof of work system is important because no one knows anyone in the blockchain. It is the cornerstone of the viability of a trust-less decentralized system where money is being minted.

Cryptocurrency features

Cryptocurrencies have come to disrupt the way we associate with money. To make it easier to understand how they work, we need to define money.

Money is a means of exchange. To spend physical money, you need to prove to everyone that you have paper or coin money, that it is genuine, and that you own it. We can refer to this as a public database of fiat money. Once you spend it, you transfer it to another person, and now they can prove they own it. This is essentially the same with cryptocurrencies.

So, what makes cryptocurrencies different from fiat currencies?

It is virtually impossible to fake transactions

Blockchain balances are more secure than bank balances. This is because it is not possible to fake the private keys that each holder of the coins signs every transaction with, for miners to confirm the authenticity of the transaction.

Security in the verification of transactions

Because they are consensus-based, a selected number of nodes must assess the veracity of a transaction before it can be added to a block. If the majority of nodes confirm that the transaction is valid, it is added to the blockchain. This is more secure than having a centralized system where bank balances can be changed without the account holders' authority.

Anonymous transactions

You do not need to put your real identity to your account to be a bitcoin holder. The keys used to identify accounts are random chains, usually of 30 characters in length. This provides anonymity, which no other money system in the world has.

Absence of intermediaries

Transacting in cryptocurrencies is unregulated. You don't need permission from anyone to use them. The software is open source and free. You just download it, buy or mine the currency, and you can use it as you deem fit.

It is fast and borderless

Confirmations in blockchain ledgers are done immediately. This means that within minutes, your transfers or purchases will be confirmed. Since this is done by a network of computers which are distributed randomly across the globe, it is indifferent to where you or your recipient is. The system is global and fast.

Irreversible transactions

Once confirmed, transactions cannot be reversed. They are locked in the blockchain forever.

Low cost of transfers

Transfers happen in blockchain at a small fraction of the fees that happen in the fiat currency world. This is because the technology is peer to peer, and there are no intermediaries. Transaction fees are entirely voluntary, and are demand driven. When miners discover blocks, they will confirm the transactions that offer them higher fees. However, the fees are still retained at a very small fraction of transferring fiat.

For example, LocalBitcoin.com has introduced a system that will make it possible to carry out deposits at the cost of 0.00066BTC per deposit and 0.00022BTC per transfer. This implies that, for example, if you are sending $10,000 worth of Bitcoin, you will incur almost as much as you will when sending $1,000,000 because the transfer is dependent on the fee you propose to pay, and how acceptable it is to the miners.

Controlled supply

Most block chains have a predetermined amount of cryptocurrency that cannot be changed, and a frequency of which it is availed. This means that there can be no surprise minting, inflation, etc.

Balances are more realistic than bank balances

When you take money to a bank, someone tells you that they have a certain amount of money in your account. It means they have your debt. A bank statement can, therefore, be described as an intent by the bank to pay you the balance. It is a debt statement. Cryptocurrencies are reflective of what you have. No one is holding it on your behalf. It is there in your wallet, true and available.

The potential of smart contracts

Blockchain technology is not all about cryptocurrencies. In fact, digital currencies were a by-product of the blockchain innovation. One of the greater promises of this technology is the advent of decentralized automated contracts called smart contracts.

A smart contract is a written code that holds an asset that is to be transferred to a party, based on certain conditions. After validating all the conditions, e.g., time, the deposit of an asset, or data input, it automatically executes a transfer to the other party or initiates other conditions like refunds or confirmation outputs.

Because the blockchain is decentralized, smart contracts are confirmed in the same way cryptocurrencies are, and are therefore immutable and irreversible. They act as seamless replacements of lawyers and other third parties.

For example, if you get a car on loan, a smart contract could be initiated that locks the car if you don't deposit a certain amount of payment to a certain address at a certain time of the month.

If you are paying in cryptocurrency, you could also initiate a smart contract that commands the wallet to release the amount at a particular time to the said address.

The Birth of Bitcoin

In November 2008, Satoshi Nakamoto, an individual or group of cryptographers who have managed to remain anonymous, released the Bitcoin white paper to a cryptography mailing list.

It detailed an ingenious method of creating a peer-to-peer, online, cashless electronic transaction system that depended on consensus confirmation, and not on trust.

The protocol was released on January 3rd, 2009, and bitcoin went on to be regarded as the first digital cryptocurrency. There were other previous attempts at electronic money, but they all failed the decentralization test, which is a key function of cryptocurrencies as it protects the currency from regulation and control.

Satoshi himself remains anonymous, but the first people to adopt the coin are well known. The first Bitcoin transaction was done by Satoshi himself, where he sent 10 BTC to Hal Finney, the developer of the Reusable Proof of Work algorithm.

The best well-known face of Bitcoin is Gavin Andresen, who runs the Bitcoin Foundation.

At first, only people in the cryptography world could use the bitcoin, before they generated enough publicity to grow a community of users.

The value of the BTC was originally set by negotiation between two parties before a transaction. One of the most famous transactions of Bitcoin was that of a purchase of two pizzas from Papa John's for a negotiated price of 10,000 BTC by a developer known as Laszlo Hanyecz. Today, that would be equivalent to $35,000,000!

Ways of Obtaining and Storing Bitcoin

Mining

To maintain a slow and steady rate of generating bitcoins, a Proof of Work method is built into the program. Miners have to find random blocks whose value is lower than or equal to a set value.

A maximum of only 2016 blocks can be mined roughly every two weeks, which translates to about a block every 10 minutes. Every time a block is mined, a reward is given to the miner. This reward is halved every four years, meaning that by the time the last of the 21 million bitcoin is mined, the reward will be very close to zero.

Miners also earn transaction fees that are voluntarily given by bitcoin users to confirm transactions and embed them into the blockchain.

Each computer has to put in work to discover a valid hash for a block in the network.

With the hash, they can enjoin the new block to the most recent block in the chain. The block is then propagated to the entire network, and a bitcoin reward claimed.

Every transaction must be confirmed by a miner, embedded in a block, and propagated as an update to every other peer node in the blockchain.

Once this is done, the record is immutable. It cannot be changed by anyone, and it is a permanent part of the blockchain.

Building a trust-based consensus on the blockchain to create value

To regard anything as money, anyone who intends to exchange it for valuable goods must be satisfied with a few conditions:

- **That the supply of this money is scarce**. This creates a motivating factor to have some of it because as its demand increases, it will increase so much in value that they may not be able to afford it.
- **That everyone will accept it as money**. This is important so that it is possible to later convert it into valuable things when you need them.
- **That once it is transferred, it is gone**. This will give confidence that it cannot be copied, and, therefore, remains scarce.
- **That to get it, you have to part with something of equal value**. Which is why computers have to prove they worked to mint new coins.
- **That having parted with it, you no longer have it**. which makes it impossible to copy.
- **That once you acquire it, everyone agrees you have it**. which makes it possible to use it later.

With a decentralized system, there is no element of a third party, and everything done on the network is passed by consensus. The element of trust is replaced by distributed consensus. In other words, the people in the community exercise their power directly, all the time. This presents a problem, as information generated by one node after a transaction must reflect consistently and accurately in all the other nodes.

This is achieved in two ways:

- **Strict Consistency**, where confirmation is done in a slow process, which allows for the information to spread to the whole network.
- **Eventual Consistency**, where the transactions are immediately confirmed, but a rider is retained by the transacting node to cancel it if it gets rejected by other nodes.

The complexity of proof of work

Because of the ever-improving computing power being employed by miners, the bitcoin protocol has to compensate by raising the complexity of the proof of work algorithm. This helps keep the hash rate steady. Nowadays, a lot of computing power, electricity, and time is required to mine any meaningful quantities of bitcoin.

Originally, ordinary home computers could be used to do mining. In 2013, a Chinese firm produced the first ASIC (Application Specific Integrated Circuits) graphics cards specifically for data mining. These cards could mine bitcoin 50 times faster than normal graphics cards, and the age of mining "farms" and "pools" began.

It is, therefore, uneconomical at the current time to try and mine bitcoin using a desktop or laptop at home.

Mining Pools

If still interested in mining, and with no meaningful computing power, you can still join a mining pool. This increases the collective hash rate, and allows one to pay "rent" for mining power. However, you should note that mining is no longer as profitable as it used to be.

There are some quite famous pools, including AntPool, BTC.com, BTC.Top, Bixin, F2Pool, and BTCC.

However, the consensus is simple. Buy Bitcoin or whatever altcoin, and trade wisely to grow your portfolio!

Mining Pyramids

Another good reason to keep off pool mining is that it has also seen an increase in pyramid schemes masquerading as mining pools. They use different tactics to con people out of their money.

If you must join a mining cloud, confirm several ups and downs of whichever pool you want to join to avoid disappointment.

Characteristics of a mining pool scam

- The moment you post your Bitcoin, you are at a total risk of losing it. So only post what you are prepared to lose.
- Don't trust anyone because they simply have a website. Anyone can create a website.
- You will only make a profit when you draw out all your initial investment to a safe wallet.
- If your figures keep increasing and you cannot draw them out of the system, they are probably just figures, and you may never get them. They are supposed to draw you out to spend more and set you up for a spectacular con game.

- There are no fast rewards. This is a big sign there is a con game in the offing.
- If you have to pay licenses, your chance of recovering that money is pushed further down the calendar.

Proof that a mining pool is genuine

- They have an exchange license in the country they are operating.
- Real addresses where they allow you to visit and audit the mine.
- Authentic personalities
- A proper certificate of incorporation, and bank accounts that are registered in the name of the company.
- Provable hashing power; this is the fact that the mine will be able to generate as many bitcoins as will make your investment, and that of others, worthwhile.

Some of the most prominent mining farms include mininghub.io, Airbitz, ANX and BitInstant and BTCS Inc.

Buying

There are three main ways in which you can buy bitcoin and any other crypto coin. You can buy it using fiat currency from a friend to your wallet, or you can find an exchange that deals in cryptocurrencies, and trade your fiat currency from your bank account for the cryptocurrency. You can also buy bitcoin from a bitcoin ATM.

Buying from stock exchanges

While the most immediate and secure way of starting and growing your portfolio is to buy, the market has its fair share of fraudsters who operate as brokers and exchange agencies of cryptocurrencies.

But let us look at the best-established exchange platforms from across the world.

Country	Platform
United States	itBit, Gemini, Coinbase
United Kingdom	Bittylicious, Coincorner, Coinfloor
China	OkCoin, Uhobi
Japan	BitFlyer, BTCBox, Coincheck
India	Coinsecure, Unocoin, Zebpay
South Korea	Coinone, Korbit, Bithumb

More of this can be found on https://bitcoin.org/en/exchanges.

Let us have a look at several of the international exchange platforms and how they operate:

Coinbase

Founded in June 2012, with headquarters in San Francisco, California, Coinbase runs an exchange which accepts fiat currency for bitcoin, Litecoin, and Ethereum, and also trades between cryptocurrencies.

It accepts legal tender from 32 countries, and has a bitcoin wallet that is operable in 190 countries across the globe.

Coinbase exchanges can be effected through a bank transfer. When on the platform, you can trade either as a "taker" where you pledge a fee of 0.25%, or as a "maker," where you offer no fee.

LocalBitcoins

Also founded in June 2012, LocalBitcoins has its headquarters in Helsinki, Finland. Essentially, it is a marketplace which operates an escrow-based protection program to ensure that money is not lost when it is transferred for buying or selling currencies.

People post their intent to sell or buy the coin, and for how much of the resident fiat currency. Those who want to do business with any posted intent will agree to pay cash for cryptocurrencies, or through online transfer.

LocalBitcoins has had its fair share of frustrations with the legal mechanisms of different countries, but its trader base continues to grow.

The site has a dispute resolution mechanism to mitigate conflicts between buyers and sellers.

Bitsquare

Bit Square operates a desktop application that allows you to trade your fiat currency to bitcoin, bypassing many challenges that you may encounter with other exchanges.

The site promises a simple installation and operation that can be done within 10 minutes.

Kraken

Operating mainly in Canada, Europe, Japan and the United States, Kraken is touted as one of the most transparent and secure bitcoin exchanges in the market. They are currently overseeing the Mt. Gox scam bitcoin claims.

It currently has the biggest EUR to cryptocurrency trading volume in the world. They also accept the Canadian dollar and the GBP, with no minimum deposit set to trade.

They offer bitcoin and Ethereum trading, among other cryptocurrencies, and are pioneers in cryptographic platform audit standards. They also have a "maker" and "taker" system where they charge different fees.

BitStamp

Bitstamp claims to offer cold storage for 98% of the portfolio put on their platform, which is a first step in the right direction to assure the safety of funds, especially after they were hacked in 2015.

With offices in Luxembourg, New York, and London, they claim to be the first fully licensed cryptocurrency operator in Europe.

Their platform accepts fiat deposits directly for exchange into cryptocurrencies via bank transfer, but does not do instant payments like PayPal or MasterCard.

Bittrex

Bittrex is one of the newest exchanges, and they are prominent on security and speed. Built in the U.S., they promise fast and easy deposits and withdrawals, while guaranteeing the unrivaled quality of service and security.

All trading fees are set at a flat rate of 0.25%.

Poloniex

With over 80 coins on its platform, Poloniex is one of the biggest and most diverse crypto exchanges in the world. It has a double verification account opening system for security purposes.

Based in San Francisco, California, the exchange was established in January 2014, by Trista D'Agosta, and does not accept fiat currency. However, it has a very smart trading screen, and a very transparent fee structure based on the taker/maker model. The makers have a higher fee, and lenders are charged a flat 15% on interest.

Also, due to the volume of trading on the platform, it tends to be slow, and their support can be quite frustrating.

Bithumb

This is a little-known cryptocurrency exchange that is generating very intense Bitcoin Cash, Ethereum, Litecoin, and Bitcoin to fiat exchange traffic. Other coins on offer at this exchange include the Dash, Litecoin, Ripple, ETC, and Monero. It is only providing a Korean Won fiat exchange, which is understandable if the traffic they already have is anything to go by.

Based in South Korea, it is the largest cryptocurrency exchange in a country that oscillates between third and fifth in digital asset trading in the world.

Though, it doesn't support a BTC/ETH trading pair. Bithumb has developed bitcoin gift vouchers, with the smallest fiat value being around 10,000 KRW. It also accepts them back to change into an equivalent bitcoin value.

Curiously, it is the world's biggest exchange for Bitcoin Cash, Litecoin, Ethereum, Ripple, and Dash, displaying a very interesting trend in altcoin interest in the East.

Bitfinex

If you want to trade as a corporation, Bitfinex is the place to go. This is because it allows margin trading, has very good trading rates, and boasts a huge lender market. It has among the largest amount of crypto traffic in the world. Founded in 2012, by Raphael Nicolle, and based in Hong Kong, the exchange has a primary focus on crypto traffic from the U.S.

Their security features seem to be top-notch, but like anything else on the net, they have lost millions of dollars to hackers, especially during the August 2016, heist in which 120,000 Bitcoins worth around $72 million at the time were lost.

However, they immediately issued their own token (BFX) to affected customers as security, and have since managed to buy back all the BFX for BTC, which has made them among the most trusted exchanges in existence.

Methods of storing Bitcoin

When you purchase your digital asset, you want to first identify how you want to move it across the storage methods you choose to use to hold your portfolio. You can either choose cold or hot wallets at different times, depending on your activity.

A hot wallet is an online wallet, and it is reputed to be less secure than a cold wallet, which is an offline wallet that you can use as a bank "vault" for long-term holding of your digital asset.

Any wallet you choose has two sets of keys. They are called public and private keys. The public key is the one that gives your wallet an identity to the rest of the blockchain. It is the one people send money to.

The private key is the one you use to authorize transactions from your wallet. If you lose it, you lose your wallet. You cannot get the digital assets back. Some wallets allow you to keep your private key with you offline, and some keep it online. By selecting a wallet, you agree to manage the private key for how that particular wallet is designed, and this is an important decision.

You can hold your digital assets on your personal computer, cold wallets, online wallets, and in stock exchanges.

Some wallets are multisig, meaning they require several signatures to access. They are ideal for joint ventures and family accounts. Wallets also differ in the number and type of currency they are capable of storing.

Another feature that differs between wallets is their capability to change multi-assets within the same wallet. It is an important feature to look out for when choosing a wallet.

Desktop Computer

If you want that old computer that sits offline at home to do something useful, you can use it as a desktop cold wallet for your cryptocurrency.

The best way of securing the wallet is to ensure that the desktop is always offline. Wallets that operate on desktops are super easy to use, you get to keep your private keys, and you can increase security by using a TOR system.

However, beware of computer maintenance people, being tempted to go online with the device, and viruses. Backing up the wallet is also very important to protect the assets if the computer dies.

Mobile Wallet

With mobile wallets, you can move around with them on your mobile device, and they are not entirely online wallets.

They can use the device camera to scan QR codes for public addresses. You can operate the wallet on the go, and you can use a TOR service for increased security.

However, they are as risky as the devices they are on. Recovering the asset is hard if a device is stolen. They can also be attacked by viruses and malware.

Examples are Mycelium, Copay, Jaxx, and BreadWallet.

Online Wallets

You can access some wallets through the internet. They are reputed to be riskier than offline wallets.

Advantages:

- You may find some that can be directly integrated to exchanges and are therefore important for holding of small amounts of cryptocurrency that you want to use for trading.
- They are ideal for holding small amounts of digital assets.
- They are fast with very little lag between a transaction and confirmation.

Disadvantages:

- They are hack fodder, easy to phish, and can be prone to insider hacking and malware attacks.
- The figure you see on an online wallet is just like a bank balance. You don't have it. It is with a third party.
- So long as you are online, you can be attacked by anyone using viruses and phantom programs.

So, if you must use an online wallet, keep your antivirus up-to-date, avoid suspicious sites, and do regular scans.

There are many examples of online wallets. Exchange wallets like Bittrex or QuadrigaCX, and other wallets like GreenAddress and Coins.ph.

Paper Wallets

These are the most secure methods of storing cryptocurrencies. They are more secure against hacking and can be kept safely in bank vaults or safe deposit boxes.

However, they are not ideal for moving the money around, especially for transactional purposes, and they need you to be more tech savvy to understand and use.

You can make a paper wallet with Bitcoin Armory or Bitaddress.org.

Hardware Wallets

These gadgets are rare to find because they are always in demand. They are more cumbersome than mobile or desktop wallets. Some require batteries. Others have screens which makes it very good for backing up without getting online.

Examples are Trezor, Ledger, and KeepKey.

The Chequered Rise of Bitcoin

If the story of bitcoin is anything to go by, then we are living in interesting times because then it means that some altcoins will leverage the awareness and lessons learned through the ups and downs experienced by bitcoin.

And the ride has not been pretty at times. Bitcoin has demonstrated that at this formative stage in the life of cryptocurrencies, the digital assets can depreciate when they get attacks from hackers, regulators, and pundits, and also when regulatory efforts seem to stifle their unchecked use.

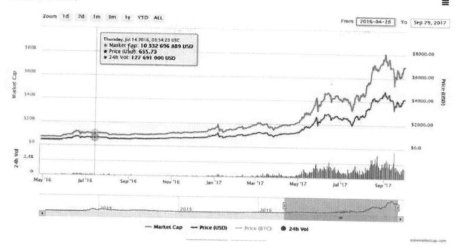

As much as they show the biggest jumps in revenue generation, no one is completely sure which coins will survive the test of time, but as of now, the bitcoin has shown that it can surpass even the biggest enthusiasts' predictions in the wake of these turbulent developments.

A quick juxtaposition of the prices exhibited by Bitcoin can help understand this. If you take the price hikes and falls as indicated in https://coinmarketcap.com/ (above, and in the table below), you can try to find out the bitcoin news around the time, and find that there is an explanation for almost every significant hike and drop.

But one thing is clear. The demand is rising for Bitcoin, and government activity, either positive or negative, quickly affects the price.

Date	Bitcoin Value (in USD)	Event
14/01/2016	431.76	Mike Hearn initiates the 'Hearnia' by Quitting bitcoin. Bitcoin drops $50 in 10 days
24/01/2016	397.92	The negative effects 'Hearnia's' effect unfolds
21/02/2016	439.84	Consensus in Hong Kong to support Segwit and initiate the hard fork
02/02/2016	433.16	The Divided Round Table Consensus effect unfolds
04/04/2016	420.61	OpenBazaar, a virtual mall with peer to peer capability, opens
14/04/2016	426.28	The positive effect of the openbazaar news
02/05/2016	447.64	Craig Wright claims in a blog that he is Satoshi Nakamoto
12/05/2016	454.36	The fake Satoshi news causes a surge in bitcoin price
09/07/2016	652.12	The Second Halving reduces block mining rewards to 12.5 BTC
19/07/2017	674.03	The Bitcoin price suffers no effect as a result of halving

02/08/2016	594.86	Bitfinex gets hacked loosing almost 120,000 BTC price drops by almost $100 the same day
12/08/2016	591.36	Bitcoin Survives the Bitfinex hack, and the drop in price is recovered
09/09/2016	726.36	Donald Trump ascends to office, and traditional markets plummet
19/09/2016	749.1	Bitcoin exhibits a positive growth as a result of other markets' plunge
03/01/2017	1020.47	Bitcoin breaks the $1,000 mark for the first time
13/01/2017	806.94	The checkered development continues
10/03/2017	1201.86	The Winkelvos brothers are denied a license by the SEC to form a Bitcoin Exchange.
20/03/2017	1037.1	Bitcoin takes a plunge that could be related to the SEC Story
01/04/2017	1085.03	Japan declares bitcoin as a legal tender
10/04/2017	1215.7	Bitcoin starts a robust climb after Japan News
08/01/2017	2787.85	The Hard Fork Happens, creating Bitcoin Cash

18/08/2017	3383.79	Bitcoin continues a brave climb riding on the publicity created by the hard fork
01/09/2017	4892.01	Bitcoin's popularity continues to soar; then China announces a crackdown on exchanges
16/09/2017	3716.32	The China ban and a scathing attack from JP Morgan sees Bitcoin witness the largest decline in its history
29/09/2017	4130.99	Bitcoin survives again and is on the mend.

To be continued...

You will find that there is a direct correlation between bad news and price drops, but Bitcoin prices seem to always recover.

Another interesting aspect arises where the bitcoin appreciates in value due to uncertainties surrounding fiat currencies as can be seen in November 2016 when markets plummeted as a result of the defeat of Hilary Clinton by Donald Trump.

Bitcoin Risks

Cryptocurrency is not always a walk in the park. The original blockchain on which bitcoin is based has not been spared its fair share of problems, and this has either affected its price, required major upgrades, or even caused community splits.

There have been several problems with the blockchain itself, especially about hacking, consensus problems and potential embezzling as we will see here.

The Mt. GOX hack

In February 2014, the biggest bitcoin exchange in the world, operating from Shibuya, Japan, closed all operations and filed for protection against customer debt. They had just lost 850,000 bitcoins (around 7% of the volume traded at Mt. GOX) to a fraudulent hack. There was also a nominal drop of the bitcoin to the price of a penny which lasted minutes but which allowed for massive "asks." Initial indications pointed to a possible embezzlement scheme by the proprietor. He was a French national working out of Japan, known as Mark Kapelês.

He was arrested by Japanese authorities in July 2015, after initial indications showed that some of the coins had been disappearing from the company's hot wallet since 2011.

He pleaded not guilty. And he was probably innocent, as most of the coins have been found with a Russian money launderer in July 2017, going by the name of Alexander Vinnik. Vinnik's connection to the leaked coins have been established, and this is a possible reason why bitcoin has survived the latest Chinese and Wall Street attacks to register massive gains in value.

In October 2011, there was a bitcoin leak to unregistered addresses, which were a part of this hack. This was a bug that was discovered by the developers later and sealed. Members of the community seem to be confident that such hacks have been effectively defeated.

The news of the recovery must have galvanized the community, that it was not possible to loot the cryptocurrency, no matter how long you ran.

The Cryptocurrency Ecosystem

There are many currencies in existence. By July 2017, more than 900 coins were in the market. All coins available in the market have unique properties, depending on the software they operate. The following are the top 10 currencies in operation, based on the market capitalization as tabulated by CoinMarketCap.

Ether

Built by the Ethereum foundation, a Swiss not-for-profit organization, the Ether is described as a fuel for their blockchain. The Ethereum blockchain is designed to run smart contracts.

The coin allows users to pay for services like rewards to machines on which the network runs, and pay the developers of the smart contracts and the transaction fees.

It first emerged on the market in August 2014, in the presale that funded the project.

The beauty about the Ethereum blockchain is that it is a massive improvement of the Bitcoin Core, in that it allows automatic, executable, and inalterable contracts to run on it.

Since the platform is open source, it allows for the integration of applications developed by all manner of concept development ideas, who can also operate their crypto coins with a myriad of properties.

The Ethereum platform has ushered in a new era of blockchain with smart contracts that can be used to run databases for hospitals, banks, libraries, registries, and even countries. Conditions in smart contracts are clear, once the contract is accepted - the rest is performed automatically, so it is not a surprise that Ethereum became the largest platform for future ICOs where Ether is the coin used as a fuel for accessing the blockchain. It places the Ether at an advantage to have an ever-increasing demand as the fuel for accessing the blockchain.

Bitcoin Cash

Due to problems with the backlogs in confirming transactions on the main bitcoin network as explained in section10.3, the community decided to initiate a user activated hard fork (UAHF), essentially creating a new blockchain, with a new coin known as Bitcoin Cash (BCH).

This fork was done on August 1, 2017. Anyone who had Bitcoin in their private wallets received a similar number of BCH as a result.

Ripple

Ripple is the coin developed by Ripple Labs, Inc. to enable banks and other financial institutions to quickly and very cheaply transfer money across the world.

It fuels the Ripple transaction protocol, which also allows for the transfer of any currency between any two entities.

The protocol was conceived based on concepts developed in 2004 by Ryan Fugger, a resident of Vancouver, British Columbia. He surrendered the concepts to Jeb McCaleb and Chris Larsen, who, in May 2011, developed the decentralized system called Ripple. The network works by consensus verification by members of the network, and this is reputed with a decrease in the fees required to transact, the wait time, and amount of electricity used by the network.

Litecoin

 Charlie Lee, who formerly worked for Google, released Litecoin on October 7, 2011. While most of the network's features resemble those of bitcoin, Litecoin boasts almost free transactions, use of SegWit, an increased number of coins and a "lightning network".

It uses open source cryptography to create and transfer coins. No central authority controls it, and it prides itself on being four times faster than Bitcoin.

Dash

 This is the first ever decentralized autonomous network, meaning that it is a company that is run by the community with no central. It offers all the features of Bitcoin, but with advanced features like InstantSend, PrivateSend, and Decentralized Governance.

It was released as XCoin or Darkcoin on January 18, 2014, by Evan Duffield, and was designed on a two-tier architecture. This means that there are two types of nodes that power the network, with some acting as miners and others as the custodians of the advanced features mentioned above.

Nem

This currency is an open source code base written entirely in Java and created by a person who likes hiding his true identity but is known as UtopianFuture.

Its stated goal is wide distribution, and it introduces the concept of Proof of Importance. It was launched on March 21, 2015. It is characterized by constant bug removal updates, but it has a major update called Catapult coming up to improve the network's stability and versatility.

It is closely associated with Tech Bureau, the corporate owner of the major cryptocurrency exchange platforms in Japan.

What to check before buying and trading Bitcoin

The Good

In a nutshell, you can make money in buying and trading bitcoin and altcoins.

A whole lot of money. This is more so if you look at the whole cryptocurrency landscape and keep on learning the art of speculative short-term trading, or hold those currencies you think will hold their own and keep rising in value.

The Bad

Pumps and Dumps

Scammers have jumped onto the bandwagon of cryptocurrency to make money using pumps and dumps. When a coin is being pumped, someone gets onto its exchange using multiple identities, and acquires a sizeable amount of the coin. They then create hype about the coin using activity on the main exchanges, fake news, blog posts, or even word of mouth to initiate a buying frenzy.

Once the buying craze hikes the price to a desired level, and buyers are knocking on the door, the scammer dumps his stocks at the high price. By the time everyone else notices the abundant supply and drops the bid price, the scammer has dumped his coin on the high and made off with a tidy sum

Ponzi Schemes

Ponzi Schemes are among the most common scams in which you could lose your hard-earned money to people who never intend to give your money back. They work by encouraging people to recruit other people. In cryptocurrency, the recruits bring money as 'licenses' to do things like mining, and then they are promised to get their money back if they recruit other people.

Once your money is in, you will be paid small amounts from your pyramid of recruits, and, if possible, you will be enticed to plow even that into 'mining rent' to earn even more.

If you are not able to pull your money out as soon as you join, you are probably in a Ponzi scheme.

The Ugly

ICO Scams

People have become clever. In coming up with ideas that appeal to you, regarding how scalable and profitable they can be if their white paper is implemented, they will convince you to buy their coins. But you might soon realize that they never intended to carry out the white paper opportunity to fruition.

And because the blockchain is unregulated, this is a crowdfunding headache that even governments are grappling with. In the case of China, the government has decided to err on the side of caution to protect their citizens and closed down major exchanges who were also hosting ICO activity.

You have to ensure that you have done your homework to ensure you are not scammed in this way.

Find out whether they have a plausible opportunity. Is the team developing the technology verifiable? Do they have email addresses that are working? Are they known? Do they have valid registration and licenses in the countries where they are based?

Understand the blockchain that is fuelled by the coin you want to buy. Who else is buying it? What does it promise? What is new about it? What has happened to other coins that purported to do whatever this one is claiming to want to do? What will make it increase its popularity?

For example: If you want to start working with Ethereum, you could visit the following site: https://www.cryptocompare.com/coins/xrp/overview.

On this site, it is possible to assess the current position of how the coin is comparing to select fiat or other cryptocurrencies;

This picture shows that on a material day, 1 Ether is exchanging at $296.51, and it is on an upward trend of 1.17%.

You could decide to visit any of the suggested or researched reputable exchanges and either buy the Ether on the decline to hold for speculation or to cut your losses at the current exchange by dumping the coin at the current price.

You could also simply move on by selecting other currencies you might want to buy or sell. Your selection of the wallet and the exchange you choose is what will dictate what makes this possible.

Fraud

Phantom wallets, fake exchanges, and fake cryptocurrency brokers have mushroomed in the cryptocurrency boom in the last few years. Using world-renowned platforms, though not completely devoid of risk, will at least assure you that you have an acceptable amount of risk.

By choosing your wallet carefully, you can secure the bulk of your savings and only take the amount you want to exchange to the platforms you choose.

Crime

Criminals have now realized that cryptocurrencies are extremely secure, and are a more valid store of value, in many instances, than fiat currency. They will do everything possible to prise your portfolio away from you.

What are the properties of the exchange you are using? How secure is your cold storage? What would happen if your device got lost? Remember, for mobile wallets, if you lose your mobile device and you have not backed up your wallet, you have lost your portfolio. Your savings are gone. Forever! There is no system for recovery of private keys!

Governments and Bitcoin: Prohibit or Lead

Japan

When Coincheck announced that it had acquired the license to operate as a legitimate "virtual currency exchange" in Japan on September 13, 2017, the cryptocurrency fraternity heaved a huge collective sigh of relief. One of the biggest world economies had just endorsed the currency after it had received huge publicity blows from China and the U.S. in the preceding days.

This followed the official recognition that Japan accorded to the Bitcoin on April 1, 2017, as a form of payment. Japan did this to protect the users of cryptocurrencies, and formalize usage, hence ushering in a hugely needed boost to the industry.

The U.S.

The U.S. could be making concerted efforts to ensure that corporates and individuals do not hide money in crypto assets, but, in so doing, could be educating the masses on the true power of cryptocurrency.

When the IRS asked Coinbase to release cryptocurrency usage information for all unknown users for the years 2013-15, it became clear that governments were waking up and taking notice. When a critical mass of a country's economy threatens to move from the traditional markets to the blockchain, regulators have to wake up and smell the coffee.

And while this may be disappointing to a few people who wanted to enjoy the anonymity provided by the blockchain and rake in untaxed profits, it is important for cryptocurrencies to be recognized by governments so that the path to mainstream acceptance becomes easier.

South Korea

Some of the most intense cryptocurrency activity is found in South Korea. It is the fifth in the world. The Central Bank there has sensationally admitted that "cryptocurrencies and fiat currency coexist." Also, the government there is busy looking for ways of regulating cryptocurrencies.

Austria

There is a cautious approach to the adoption of cryptocurrencies by the Austrian central bank. The Governor, Mr. Ewald Nowotny, has moved from comparing the cryptocurrencies to the "Tulip Craze" of Holland of the seventeenth century, to saying that the country cannot ban them as they would a banknote.

It is now possible to exchange Euros for bitcoins from any post office in Austria.

Spain

With a declaration that bitcoin is essentially money that does not have VAT exemption, Spain has set the pace for the adoption of cryptocurrencies as a widely accepted means of exchange in Europe.

Recently, the major banks like Banc Sabadell, EVO Banc, Abanka, and Banco Popular in Spain made a deal with BTCPoint to avail over 10,000 ATMs for bitcoin to cash transactions.

Thus, with 0% commission charged on transactions, BTCPoint has entered into direct competition with Bet2Me, another exchange that charges 1% commission in the same market.

China

While China recognizes the need to take the lead in the development of blockchain technology as one of the developed economies of the world, it has recently found it necessary to rein in the advent of crowdfunding.

They have effected this clampdown with a freeze of all exchange activity on their main crypto exchanges. When BTCChina announced that they would be closing down all exchange activity from September 30, 2017, due to this, the bitcoin and all the major currencies received a massive drop in prices within days.

Real Value of Bitcoin and Other Cryptocurrencies

The jury is still out on what could happen to the value of bitcoin and any of its altcoins. Will it be adopted by the whole world? If, by 2140, when the last block is mined, there will be 20 billion humans, how much holding could they have if the bitcoin is the only currency of the world? The possibilities are mind-boggling.

The future value of Bitcoin and the altcoins

One thing is certain. With 900 plus coins in circulation, there will be wealth created and wealth lost. Most coins will fail because they are fraudulent and they have been created by people who are counting on the gullibility of the human mind when it comes to money.

Many coins will make the people who invest millions of dollars from practically nothing. If Laszlo Hanyecz did not use his 10,000 bitcoin in 2009, to buy two pizzas, he would now be worth an extra $40 million.

The other saving grace of the cryptocurrency is the simple fact that most of them are simply keys to a blockchain that performs far more important functions than the transfer of the coin that serves as the key to open it. In other words, to most of the modern-day block chains, the coin is an incidental value transfer medium. This guarantees the coin life and an ever-increasing value so long as its users continue to value the blockchain that is fuelling the coin's need.

SegWit and its impact on the market

Introduced by Dr. Peter Wuille, SegWit is the short form for Segregated witness, a controversial modification of the bitcoin blocks that frees up about 65% of block space occupied by the digital signature that confirms the presence of the digital asset, to enable a transaction involving the transfer of the bitcoins to another wallet.

With SegWit, it would mean that the Witness block is not mined but is availed to carry the signatures automatically when a block is mined.

This is controversial, in the sense that it would enlarge the blocks, and hence reduce the wait times for transactions to be embedded in blocks, a phenomenon that would reduce miners' transaction fees.

To ensure consensus, the makers of SegWit decided to try and get 95% consensus before the SegWit "soft fork" could be activated. This is so bitcoin can maintain the hash power through unanimity in implementing it, and hence stabilize and secure the blockchain.

The SegWit led to some miners leaving the bitcoin blockchain to mine altcoins and Bitcoin Cash!

Bitcoin Cash

The bitcoin block is 1MB in size, and this was done deliberately to make rogue transactions hard to carry out on the blockchain. However, as the coin became popular, legitimate transactions grew exponentially. This started affecting the speed by which miners were adding the transactions to blocks, making it necessary for people to increase fees offered to "jump the queue."

This gave rise to the "replace by fee system" which now made it possible for users to invalidate earlier transactions by duplicating them with other, more incentivized, ones. This meant that it was possible to cancel transactions, a phenomenon that should not be possible in blockchain technology if cryptocurrencies are to remain relevant as reliable forms of exchange.

Some users supported a fork, with the creation of an altcoin whose blockchain would operate on bigger blocks.

The community voted, and on August 1, 2017, Bitcoin Cash was created through a "hard fork." This essentially meant that a new coin would have to be created, as the rules no longer held for the original bitcoin due to change of the size of the blocks, and the incompatibility that would result with historical transactions.

Whoever had bitcoins before the hard fork was given a similar number of Bitcoin Cash.

The Future of Bitcoin and the Blockchain

The Blockchain of the future

So, what is the future of the Blockchain? Already, there are thousands of proposals involving blockchain technologies in various industries across the world. Bitcoin has the potential of becoming the first true currency of the world.

Peer to peer transactions could become possible the world over using the bitcoin to ensure that costs of transfer of funds are brought down. This could change the future of global banking, and, indeed, global trade.

Changing the World

A few scenarios would help in taking a peep at the future of the blockchain and what the technology could bring to the world.

Voting:

Imagine an identity revolution that gives every citizen of a country a unique identifier that has one private voting wallet. Imagine then, a smart contract that will only allow that one "vote" to only transmit from that particular wallet to the main electoral body wallet identified for each participant in a voting contest.

We could easily start voting from anywhere in the world for contestants back home, and results would instantly be visible for total votes cast for each contestant on national television!

And because it is the blockchain, the security features would remove the need for third-party transmission and verification as the system would be trust-less! We would remove the unnecessary and expensive recounts, petitions, and re-election.

Land Registration:

If the blockchain made it possible to check the provenance of deeds, in a publicly verified and traceable manner, land disputes would be eliminated in an instant.

Eradication of Food Fraud

If a technology were to be created that encodes the identity of a food product onto a label, downstream adulteration would be eliminated.

Martin Rosulek has quoted Richard Branson to have said:

"Virgin Galactic is a bold entrepreneurial technology. It's driving a revolution. And Bitcoin is doing just the same when it comes to inventing a new currency."

Who's next? Other High Potential Cryptocurrencies

So, what have we learned from the nature of the featured altcoins? What is hidden in the other hundreds of coins that exist? Why is each of them unique in its way? Which penny crypto holds a secret to future greatness? A few interesting mentions come to mind.

Ether

This is the fuel that unlocks Ethereum, the incredible smart contract hosting platform. Thousands of applications are being created to ride on

Ethereum, and the key is the Ether, even though each application can have its value.

Ripple

As much as the coin is still trading in the lower brackets regarding price, it is the power behind the Real Time Gross Settlement (RTGS) used by banks to transfer large amounts of money, cheaply, fast, across the globe. It, therefore, emerges that banks are using the same technology they don't want us to use!

If the ripple is still trading at a fraction of a dollar, then assessing its trend in the future should be interesting, especially because, by market capitalization, it is still top 10.

Litecoin

Litecoin was founded in 2011, by Charlie Lee as light-weight alternative of Bitcoin. Besides that it was a fork from Bitcoin code, it has some differences which allow it to proceed transactions faster and spend less power than Bitcoin.

Its network is more flexible – with 75% activation threshold, Segwit was activated 3 months earlier than in the Bitcoin network with 95% activation threshold. It is one of the most stable and enduring currencies due to several factors:

- It has an abundant supply, which makes it relatively reachable to beginners, and maintains a street-level exchange potency.
- Due to its endurance, it commands excellent trust as a means of exchange, and is accepted by an increasingly large number of businesses across the world.
- Its algorithm tries to address the problem of specialized hardware in mining it, which is good news for smaller mining efforts.

In the future, it is planned to introduce new features that will be integrated into Litecoin first. Among them there are the cross-chain atomic swap and the Lightning Network. Cross-chain atomic swap allows you to exchange your accounts into another cryptocurrency directly, without intermediaries and exchanges. This means that you can pay by Litecoins where they are not accepted, for example, in terminals that accept only Bitcoins. The implementation of the Lightning Network will allow for instant payments between two users. The combined use of these two functions can solve the problem of slow transactions in the Bitcoin network via the Litecoin network and will make Litecoin even more popular, and increase its cost.

Dash

The main feature that makes the Dash an appealing cryptocurrency to have, is its obsession with the anonymity of transactions. The Darksend system, which is the main innovation of the coin, is a system in which the blockchain utilizes specially designated computers to mask transactions against external verification by carrying out several transactions at once.

Unlike other coins, the Dash has no public ledger. It uses the X11 algorithm, a good alternative, that allows users with less hash power to get an opportunity to earn from transaction verification, and actually use 30% less power from other alternatives.

Monero

Just like Dash, the Monero is a study in intricate cryptography that allows it to guarantee a high level of transaction and portfolio anonymity.

With stealth addresses, transactional fractionation, and ring signatures for mixing transactions and obscuring the identity of addresses, its anonymity claim is deemed to be based on a very strong foundation.

This makes it an ideal altcoin for Darknet payments, e.g. for drugs.

Monero keeps on having increasing block sizes as its demand increases, and this can have a huge effect on its stability and overall success because processing fees and speeds keep changing with time.

NEM

Among the unique features that make NEM (XEM) a unique cryptocurrency is the application of its blockchain to other uses apart from the transfer of value, its block time, its Proof-of-Importance (POI) Algorithm, and the design of its wallet.

You don't mine blocks in the XEM blockchain. You "harvest," but only if you have in excess of 10,000 XEM in your wallet. Interestingly, you can also delegate harvesting. Whenever a new block is harvested, it is added to the blockchain, and records can be added to it.

You can send encrypted and unencrypted messages on the NEM network without necessarily transacting NEM, but this incurs fees.

The blockchain is being tested for use in banking, where it is said to be capable of reducing banking costs by more than 90%. It also seems possible to pair the blockchain with smart contract features to offer more options for exploration in the future.

Useful links

Exchanges:

https://bitcoin.org/en/exchanges

https://www.bestchange.com/

Wallets:

To buy: www.cryptowallets.org/

Free wallets: https://freewallet.org/

ICO Calendar

https://tokenmarket.net/ico-calendar

Price Analysis Resources:

https://coinmarketcap.com/currencies

https://www.cryptocompare.com/coins/btc/analysis

Largest crypto community forum:

https://bitcointalk.org/

Conclusion

With the information that you find in this book, you are now capable of finding your way to enter into the world of owning, trading, and using cryptocurrencies.

This booklet has delved much into the nature of the blockchain, and in as simple a manner as could be used, the language that gives you a layman's peek at the geeky world of the blockchain, and makes it possible for you to understand why it is a truly revolutionary innovation has been employed.

The world is taking notice, and early adopters are either making or losing money.

Trading and speculation in cryptocurrency is not a feat for the faint-hearted. You may make money in this trade. You may find many get-rich-quick propositions from clueless fraudsters. You will probably miss many opportunities to turn penny stocks into thousands of dollars.

Whatever you do, make sure that you only invest what you can afford to lose. Pick your currency, wallet, exchange, and source of reliable information with utmost care.

Use the resources provided here for more research. Read as many books and blogs as possible to understand what is happening in the world of cryptocurrencies.

The information is out there. The choice is yours!

Postface

The cryptocurrency market is also volatile, and any information about this area needs to update. I am going to publish a series of books which helps readers to realize the main trends, features, and to facilitate earning money on Bitcoin and altcoins. Furthermore, feedback from the readers is always welcome. Let me know what you think about this book – what you liked or disliked.

For getting in touch, information about new books, or to send feedback, please use this link or qr-code:

https://goo.gl/forms/fFsKpq58kjl62jcy1